YOUR WALK

and the

STRUGGLE IT TAKES

By Dan Phillips

This book is dedicated to:

Christi for introducing me to God,
it is because of her that
I was able to see that God was waiting on me
and all I had to do was allow Him in

Your Walk and the Struggle it Takes

Preface

Preface

Though I am currently 52 years old, I am really only an 18-year old Christian. I believe that God did speak to me 18 years ago. Since that time, I have been doing my best to listen to Him more frequently. This has resulted in quite a bit of soul searching and Bible reading. I have taken those efforts and put them to the test with teaching Sunday School classes and speaking with pastors about many ideas and concepts.

It helps me to put my thoughts into words and to then put them to paper. It is not with arrogance that I put those words into this book. It is from a belief in sharing my discoveries with, perhaps, other people that might be searching to better their relationship with God, just like I am. And, besides, the Holy Spirit is moving me to get this book out there for some reason!

When asked what to do with all of the messages and opportunities I hear from the Holy Spirit, a teacher once told me, "Just say YES to everything." Adopting that attitude can make a person very busy. I have, and before long, out popped this book!

This book is a compilation of several ideas in discovery. The first half of the book is about actions we might take to become more like Jesus. The second half of the book includes excerpts from a Sunday School curriculum I wrote helping us to relate to the Walk that God has invited us to take on this earth. Several of the chapters to this point will have some exercises that the reader can do to experience more of what I am trying to express. Finally, the last chapter is the current idea I am working on, and that relates to the part in each of us that is made up from God.

As one learner to another, as one walker to another, as one who struggles with the human condition, I truly hope that within these pages you find some nuggets that mean as much to you as they do to me.

Introduction

Are you a Christian?

If not, I hope that in reading this book you learn more about the philosophy of Jesus. Simply put, Jesus asks us to love one another as we would like to be loved. For Him, love means that we look for others to share love with; that we humbly serve each other, meeting their needs first; that we empathize with one another, walk a mile in their shoes; that we show our love to those not in love and encourage them to incorporate love into their lives.

If you are a Christian, what type are you? I'm not asking about Catholic versus Methodist, Presbyterian versus Baptist. I am asking if you are proactive or inactive. I am interested in Christians that believe that Christ tells us to get up and become active members in our communities, showing the love of God as our example. Jesus did not simply sit in a temple and speak with religious leaders. He walked the land, moving from place to place to be with and interact with people. Along the way, he was able to show His love. He was able to humble Himself in service. He gave the gift of God wherever He went to whomever He met. This is what Jesus wants us to do, to be active and share the love of God.

How does God speak to us?

Is God audible, can we hear Him speak? Does He only show us signs, like burning bushes? Does He answer our prayers, not in word, but in action? So many Christians will tell you in so many ways how God may or may not speak to them. There are quite a few Christians that believe that not as of yet have they heard from God. Though I believe that God did speak directly, audibly to me one time in my life, many Christians of longer or deeper faith than I are still waiting.

I encourage you to believe that God speaks to us in many ways. One of those methods is by way of opportunities. To whatever level, individually, we all have learned something about God, something about Jesus and His gifts. Not only do we know right from wrong, but we know some of the stories of the Bible, we know how Jesus would act in certain situations, we know what it is to love and to be loved.

God presents us with opportunities to demonstrate our efforts and abilities to invoke a Christ-like presence to other people in our everyday lives. We might tend to think that these kinds of opportunities are few and far between. Examples might include funerals or visits to the hospital or the birth of a child or at a wedding. Though these are quite good examples of opportunities in one's life to demonstrate Christ-like behavior, I urge you to think harder on this. We are faced with opportunities to be Christ-like or not in every moment of every day, whether with someone or alone.

- Driving on the highway and someone cuts you off
- Sitting alone at your computer and deciding whether or not to look at pornography
- Coming to a closed door with other people coming and going
- Seeing a neighbor carrying trash to the street
- Finding that once again your spouse has left his/her clothes on the floor of the closet
- Knowing that your mother-in-law sits lonely at home
- Passing a stranger in the hallway
- The man on the corner with an empty cup
- Just before dinner with the family
- A friend's child has just been hospitalized from an overdose of drugs
- Earthquake in Haiti
- Stock Market crash
- Your neighbor's house has a Foreclosure sign out front
- A power outage

Every moment of every day presents us with opportunities to listen to God. He is showing us the path on which to live our lives. Once you are in tune with this, you will hear God all day long. You will talk with God about the choices you are faced with. You will plead with God for easier ways. You will ask God for forgiveness when you choose a different path. God rewards you with more opportunities to serve and affect other people. God expands your world to encompass more people, more opportunities, more experiences, more love.

Why do bad things happen to good people?

The answer to this is a continuation of God speaking in opportunities. When you hear of bad things happening, say for example a friend of yours has got to go to the hospital; this is an opportunity for you. God is telling you that there is someone in this situation that needs the light of God to bathe them, and you are that beacon. It may be the friend, or members of their family, or it might simply be a nurse or a doctor or a hospital volunteer. But there is someone involved in this experience that needs you to show them some way to see God. You might be there to lead by example, you might be there to pray for your friend and family, or, you might be there to answer a direct question from someone about your faith. Understand that God is presenting you with an opportunity and you have the choice to respond and interact with God.

What would you like God to say to you when He meets you at the pearly gates?

This is the question that James Lipton asks every interviewee at the end of each episode of "Inside the Actors Studio." It is a question that every Christian should ask himself daily. This is a question of measurement.

It is a Christian's goal to become Christ-like. Never will any of us become Christ. We must ascertain the qualities that Jesus held and portrayed and work hard to emulate them. It is the struggle to be Christ-like that we will be measured by. When you understand that life on this earth is the place, in which we are tested, that the opportunities God puts before us are really a series of pass/fail tests, you will be able to measure your performance.

Every person we come in contact with will have some impression on them left by us. Even if we pass that stranger in a hallway and don't look up or say a word, you have left an impression. As a Christian it is our duty to leave marks of Christ on everyone we meet and live with. Leading by example is one way in which to leave a mark. But, interacting with a person, empathizing with them, introducing God into their lives, however brief, those are marks Christians leave.

The Bible has many verses that list positive and negative traits of human interaction. In reading some of these examples, remember that when you act in any of these ways, you will leave a lasting mark on the other people in that situation. It will be the compilation of these marks that will color your soul and it will be this soul that you will present to God at the pearly gates.

Immorality	Idolatry	Love
Joy	Peace	Patience
Sorcery	Jealousy	Anger
Disputes	Kindness	Goodness
Faithfulness	Gentleness	Dissention
Envy	Self-control	Tender-hearted
Forgiving	Compassion	Drunkenness
Boastful	Malice	Guile
Humility	Righteousness	Godliness
Harmonious	Hypocrisy	Slander
Greed	Competitiveness	Sympathetic
Brotherly	Give blessing	Trust

Please read Philippians 3:12 through 3:21. This is a letter from Paul. In the beginning of Chapter 3, he urges the Philippians to follow the examples of Jesus. He also tells them that all of his worldly possessions are rubbish compared to the value of following Jesus. He tells them of his faith in God.

From verse 3:12: "Not that I have already obtained *it*, or have already become perfect, but I press on..."

In this case, the italicized "*it*" may refer to the quality, or goal, of being Christ-like.

From verse 3:13: "...I do not regard myself as having laid hold of *it* yet; but one thing *I do*: forgetting what *lies* behind and reaching forward to what *lies* ahead..."

Again, he is stating that he has not yet attained the level of being Christ-like in all of his behavior. He continues to measure himself, just as we should. In so doing, he does not hold his shortcomings from the past against himself. He forgets them and continues to reach ahead. He continues to look for opportunities to perform with the same attributes as Jesus.

From verse 3:14: "I press on toward the goal for the prize of the upward call of God in Christ Jesus."

Here, Paul can see that future encounter with God at the pearly gates. He understands that our goal is to be Christ-like and that the prize for that struggle is the upward call from God.

3:15: "Let us therefore, as many as are perfect, have this attitude..."

Paul is asking us to share the same goal.

3:16: "however, let us keep living by that same *standard* to which we have attained."

Might we define "standard" as living our life with the goal of being Christ-like.

3:17-21: "Brethren, join in following my example, and observe those who walk according to the pattern you have in us. For many walk, of whom I often told you, and now tell you even weeping, *that they are* enemies of the cross of Christ, whose end is destruction, whose god is *their* appetite, and *whose* glory, is in their shame, who set their minds on earthly things. For our citizenship is in heaven, from which also we eagerly wait for a Savior, the Lord Jesus Christ; who will transform the body of our humble state into conformity with the bode of His glory, by the exertion of the power that He has even to subject all things to Himself."

Paul is telling us that he has chosen a path in life to become as Christ-like as possible. He wants us to follow the same path. He talks about the people who opt not to follow Christ and what will happen to them. He asks that we all join a citizenship of Christ-like people. This must be our goal in life, and if it were the goal of everyone, it would be a much nicer world.

Being Like Christ

Christian's Taxonomy of Emulating Christ

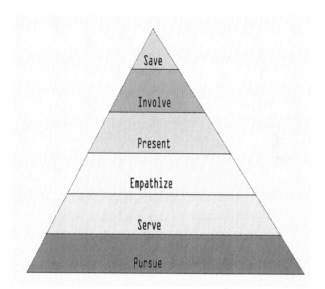

A Christian should pursue other people to demonstrate their Christ-like traits to. One cannot be an active Christian by sitting at home not incorporating one's self into the community, or the world. Key words associated with Pursue might include: to carry out, to participate in an activity, to be involved in, to quest for, and, to follow another with the intent of overtaking.

Jesus came among us to humbly serve, to cater to our needs, spoken or unspoken. Key words for Serve include: to tend to, to attend, to do for, to minister to, and, to wait upon.

Jesus was a communicator. To be effective, a communicator must deeply understand the audience. One must empathize. Empathize key words: identify with, understanding of another's situation, relate to, feel for, feel at one with, to be sensitive to, and, associate with.

As a Christian, we should strive to introduce the power and warmth of God to everyone, to every situation. We are to present God. Key words: to introduce, to make a gift of, to offer for observation, to show or display, to make known, and, acquaint.

When faced with a situation in which God is not present, a Christian must endeavor to involve Him. When the path takes you to a place where God has not been accepted, intervene and bring Him in. Key words for Involve: to include, to have as a necessary feature, to engage, to connect closely, to influence, to wrap or envelop, to comprehend, and, to subsume.

Finally, our ultimate goal is to save souls. Be the conduit, the catalyst, the gateway, that will allow God to enter another's life and save their soul. Save key words might include: to rescue from harm, to redeem, to set free from the consequences of sin, to prevent the waste or loss of, to treat with care, to deliver from misery or evil, and, to extricate from danger.

It is human nature to want to be challenged. As children, we know right from wrong, good from evil. Many a child, when finding something wonderful, will immediately look to share that with anyone they can find. They will actually go running to find people to bring the object of their wonder to. As we get older, and perhaps jaded, our excitement to share diminishes. However, as Christians, it is our responsibility to share God with anyone we can find. Many of us might be uncomfortable with any activity resembling evangelism. But, no one can argue with the fact it is our creed to work to become Christ-like. The world would be a much better place if we loved each other as we love God. Follow these steps as way to become more Christ-like.

Humble Pie

My family and I went out to dinner. My family includes my
mother-in-law, Gladys, wife, Christi, daughter, Mary, and son,
Danny. We went to this restaurant that people were talking about
called Humble Pie.

On the last day of winter, as we entered the restaurant, a
gentlemen, who later turned out to be our server, greeted us
warmly and held the door open for Gladys and the rest of us. He
looked me in the eyes and as he shook my hand, introduced
himself as Justin. He then proceeded to shake everyone's hand.
He quickly took our coats and brought them to the coat check as
we shook off the cold. Then, he escorted us to our table, taking
Gladys' arm as he spoke about the attributes of the restaurant along
the way.

Justin pulled out the table to make it easier to slide in and around.
He checked to make sure each of us was comfortable and quickly
took a drink order. The unique décor of the restaurant and the
descriptions he told us as we walked to our table had us all looking
around and before we knew it our drinks were in front of us. Justin
looked straight at Danny and asked if he could squish in next to
him and he did just that.

Justin started to ask us about our favorite meals. He started off
telling us a story of eating fried chicken at his grandmother's every
Sunday afternoon as he grew up, and that he really loved the rice
and gravy. Soon, we were all telling stories of favorite family
meals and what each of us liked. After a bit, he asked a few more
questions about our preferences or dislikes. He left the table as we
continued telling family stories, topping off our drinks with none
of us really noticing.

He came back to the table with the menus and some printouts of
the Daily Specials. If I didn't know any better, some of those

specials just coincidentally seemed to be some of the favorite meals we all were just talking about. It was a bit peculiar. Gladys ordered a house salad before her entrée and Justin remembered her story of her love of onions, so he asked her if she wanted extra onions, or a variety of Vidalia, Spanish and yellow. I picked lasagna off of the menu, without noticing that it was eggplant, a food I am allergic too. Well, Justin brought me up to speed on that oversight right away, and even suggested I try this new dish with a lemon butter sauce on Tilapia, remembering that I said I liked fish. Christi, Mary and Danny all ordered off of the specials page excited that their favorite meals were on the list.

As we were waiting for our food, I noticed that at all of the tables, everyone was happy. Drinks were all full. There were no dirty dishes to be found. Bread baskets came frequently with warm replacements. Other servers sat at the tables with their customers telling stories too. Without realizing it, an older gentleman, at another table, had dropped his napkin and his server discretely handed him a new one while picking up the dropped one. Lively conversations were going on, in between bites, at every table.

Justin brought our food and it was wonderful. Smiles were on all of our faces. He cleared the table as we finished and asked to sit down to talk about dessert. Both Mary and Danny squeezed in wanting him to sit next to them to describe the rolling table of desserts before us.

Finally, our meal was done. The bill was settled. Justin brought our coats to the table and helped the ladies on with theirs. Once again, looking each of us in the eye, he shook our hand as he bid us farewell. As we left the restaurant, opening the door to the sunny first day of spring, we felt as if we left a friend behind. Justin, his humility was genuine, his service impeccable, his attitude wonderful. We knew we would be back.

✧ ✧ ✧

Wouldn't it be wonderful if there was a Humble Pie restaurant in all of our neighborhoods?

Now, think of the hierarchy of Christ-like behavior and the examples of them throughout this story. First, Justin pursued us. He met us at the door and warmly welcomed each of us. He actively became involved in our experience. The whole story is about how he served us; from continually topping off our drinks to clearing the table and ensuring we were satisfied. He was attentive to our needs. He was a great communicator. He initiated conversation and encouraged each of us to contribute. He was empathetic, getting down to our level, sitting among us telling family stories. He presented us with the best Humble Pie had to offer. He gifted us not only with great food but with memories connected to it. When he realized that I wasn't going to like my food choice, he intervened and led me back towards a more rewarding food choice. He had enveloped my well being into his domain of service, involving what he knew about the food and my make-up and used that to influence my next choice. Finally, Justin has saved us from poor experiences at restaurants. We now know of a place to go where we are welcome, protected, and served very well. We are delivered from the misery of other, substandard restaurants.

Pursue

- To carry out
- To participate in an activity
- To be involved in
- To quest for
- To follow another with the intent of overtaking

As a Christian, our goal is to be Christ-like. What a lofty goal indeed! If you are not uncertain, or lacking in confidence, about how one such as us is to attain that goal, I dare say you are in a very small minority. Not only was Jesus so perfect in so many ways, but he also changed the world. We will cover the attributes of Jesus in later chapters. For now, let's define the term "world."

Jesus changed the world He lived in, and continues to shape the world today. If our goal is to be like Him, we need to grab a human definition of what the world means to us. Now, there are human beings that can affect the world. Hitler was an example of one. Any president of the United States would provide more examples. However, not all of us find ourselves in a position to have such an impact as a politician, a sports legend, a rock star, or, a Hollywood actor.

Your world should start with the people you know well. This could include your family, your neighbors, your work colleagues, and, your church. This should make up the basis of your world. A Christian must not limit the size of his world due to fear or lack of effort. Many people will say something like, "My job is to be the best parent to my children that I can be. I need to lead by example in the home."

While parenting is very important, it should not put limiting boundaries in your world. You need to get out of being with just your family. You need to stretch your world to friends and colleagues, and then, most importantly, beyond. Jesus walked the land, from town to town, from temple to church to synagogue. He actively pursued other people to share God with.

All of Matthew chapter 9 relates well to the act of searching for people that need God in your world. Let's start with Matthew 9:35-38:

> [35]Jesus went through all the towns and villages, teaching in their synagogues, preaching the good news of the kingdom and healing every disease and sickness. [36]When he saw the crowds, he had compassion on them, because they were harassed and helpless, like sheep without a shepherd. [37]Then he said to his disciples, "The harvest is plentiful but the workers are few. [38]Ask the Lord of the harvest, therefore, to send out workers into his harvest field."

Jesus is asking us for help. Does God expect us to heal diseases and sickness? Not by ourselves, no. But God is asking us to be the conduit to Him, to let His light shine through us to the people in our expanded world that need Him. It may not be to cure a disease, but simply to show someone that there are people in this world, people of God, that love them as they are.

In Luke chapter 15, the story of the Lost Sheep can help us to realize the importance of expanding our world. If we remain in isolation with only those souls that are saved, many will be lost.

> [1]Now the tax collectors and "sinners" were all gathering around to hear him. [2]But the Pharisees and the teachers of the law muttered, "This man welcomes sinners and eats with them."
>
> [3]Then Jesus told them this parable: [4]"Suppose one of you has a hundred sheep and loses one of them. Does he not leave the ninety-nine in the open country and go after the lost sheep until he finds it? [5]And when he finds it, he

joyfully puts it on his shoulders [6]and goes home. Then he calls his friends and neighbors together and says, 'Rejoice with me; I have found my lost sheep.' [7]I tell you that in the same way there will be more rejoicing in heaven over one sinner who repents than over ninety-nine righteous persons who do not need to repent.

From Matthew chapter 9 again, verses 1-8:

[1]Jesus stepped into a boat, crossed over and came to his own town. [2]Some men brought to him a paralytic, lying on a mat. When Jesus saw their faith, he said to the paralytic, "Take heart, son; your sins are forgiven."

[3]At this, some of the teachers of the law said to themselves, "This fellow is blaspheming!"

[4]Knowing their thoughts, Jesus said, "Why do you entertain evil thoughts in your hearts? [5]Which is easier: to say, 'Your sins are forgiven,' or to say, 'Get up and walk'? [6]But so that you may know that the Son of Man has authority on earth to forgive sins...." Then he said to the paralytic, "Get up, take your mat and go home." [7]And the man got up and went home. [8]When the crowd saw this, they were filled with awe; and they praised God, who had given such authority to men.

This story definitely shows the power and love of God. We cannot hope to achieve the same feat. But understand that as you go out into the world, people will introduce you to their friends. They may not be paralyzed, but they will have problems of their own. As you are able to help them through God, others may criticize you. Continue on your path with God and do the best you can to help those in need. Soon, those who criticized you will begin to see that there is more to you than meets the eye.

Perhaps this story from Luke chapter 5 might bring more clarity:

²⁷After this, Jesus went out and saw a tax collector by the name of Levi sitting at his tax booth. "Follow me," Jesus said to him, ²⁸and Levi got up, left everything and followed him.

²⁹Then Levi held a great banquet for Jesus at his house, and a large crowd of tax collectors and others were eating with them. ³⁰But the Pharisees and the teachers of the law who belonged to their sect complained to his disciples, "Why do you eat and drink with tax collectors and 'sinners'?"

³¹Jesus answered them, "It is not the healthy who need a doctor, but the sick. ³²I have not come to call the righteous, but sinners to repentance."

It is not the saved who need saving. We must expand our world to find those who don't know God. We are to search for them, and then in any way possible, we are to show God to them. Yes, even the healthy need looking after; meaning that you need not neglect your own family to pursue others. But, you are to expand your world in search of people that need to see some form of Christ-like behavior, and God will put you in those situations, well equipped, to do just that.

- Carry out God's wish for us to expand our world
- Participate in new activities to find others
- Get involved in your community, your church
- Quest for opportunities to meet new people
- Follow other people that you know are missing God with the intent of overtaking them to introduce them to God

✧ ✧ ✧

Exercises

1.   Define your world as it stands now. This is not so much a
     geographical exercise but a social one. List the people that
     make up those that you influence. Then, list the people that
     fit within your comfort zone, meaning that it would not be
     too much of a stretch for you to speak with them.

     _____

     _____

     _____

2.   Now consider a different world. Here, you must expand
     your world, the scope of your personal contacts. What can
     you do to meet and talk with more people in your day to
     day life; or, to make special excursions to meet new people
     in new settings? List ways in which you can expand your
     world.

     _____

     _____

     _____

3.   Within your world, indentify those that you feel are in a
     strong relationship with God. Also list the ones that don't
     presently have a healthy relationship with God. Plan your
     pursuit of these people that are struggling. How can you
     get in front of them?

     _____

     _____

     _____

4. Next, identify at least one lost sheep. This person should
    be in your expanded world. Make plans that will allow you
    to introduce yourself and to become friendlier with that
    person. You want to get to a point that you can meet and
    talk easily, maybe a lunch meeting every few weeks,
    something like that.

    _____

    _____

    _____

    _____

    _____

5. Make a list of new things you can do to get out and meet a
    new crowd of people. These activities should definitely
    take you out of your comfort zone. You might try joining a
    sports league, or a book club, or volunteering at a hospital
    or food line. Then, do the activities on your list.

    _____

    _____

    _____

    _____

    _____

6.   Does your world reflect your heart? Your heart should help you determine the scope and size of your world; your heart and the Holy Spirit.

_____

_____

_____

Serve

- To tend to
- To attend
- To do for
- To minister to
- To wait upon

For me, the easiest way to be like Christ is to serve. More often than not, the person that you serve is so genuinely happy to be so well treated that their thanks and appreciation are quite rewarding. Don't get me wrong, one does not serve another with the expectation of reward. One serves another out of love for another human being.

Most people tell me that this is a difficult task for them. In essence, they tell me that they can't get out of the way of their own ego. They can't be humble. There is no room for selfishness if one is to serve. That does not mean that you have to be selfless.

God expects you to be true to yourself. Carry your persona well. Serving others does not mean that you become a wall-flower or a doormat. God has given you fruits of the spirit. God has blessed you with the tools that you require when an opportunity arises to serve another. He asks that you incorporate humility into your personality to better serve. Consider the following quote from Bruce K. Waltke,

> "God guides us first through His Word, then through our heartfelt desires, then the wise counsel of others, and then our circumstances. At that point we must rely on our own sound judgment...God gave each of us a brain, and He expects us to put it to good use."

Being Christ-like isn't easy and perhaps this will be the first real test. We must serve others simply because we love them. But how can we love perfect strangers? We must change our mindset from worrying about potential dangers, or that we might find ourselves in an uncomfortable situation. We must push ourselves to love others because we all share the human condition. We are all on earth struggling to do our best, either to survive or to go on to heaven. There is no one person higher than another in this shared struggle, and, there should be no one lower either. Love each other because we are made in God's image and we struggle to be like Him every moment of every day. We are in this together.

Read the story of The Lord's Supper and Jesus Washes the Disciples' Feet from John 13. Then, look at verses 13-17:

> [13]"You call me 'Teacher' and 'Lord,' and rightly so, for that is what I am. [14]Now that I, your Lord and Teacher, have washed your feet, you also should wash one another's feet. [15]I have set you an example that you should do as I have done for you. [16]I tell you the truth, no servant is greater than his master, nor is a messenger greater than the one who sent him. [17]Now that you know these things, you will be blessed if you do them.

In this passage you can see that Jesus did not give up who He was. He retained His personality, His respect as teacher and Lord. However, He has also shown His humility when He states that servant or master, all are the same and all should follow His example of service. Now, since we now know that we are to serve, we are commanded to do them to receive the blessings of the Lord.

Now, look to the letter Paul wrote to the Philippians. In 1:21 he says in simple words, "to live is Christ." What a powerful statement. He has come to the realization that he wants to live as Christ lives. He sees living, not as Christ, to be so much less so as to consider dying to be with Him. In verse 24 he tells the Philippians that he understands that it is necessary for him to remain in this world to serve as an example so that God might overflow in them.

In the second chapter of Philippians, Paul encourages the Philippians to be like Christ, to imitate His humility. From Philippians 2:3-4:

> [3]Do nothing out of selfish ambition or vain conceit, but in humility consider others better than yourselves. [4]Each of you should look not only to your own interests, but also to the interests of others.

Get out of your own head. Get beyond your ego. Get past today's pervasive feeling of entitlement. Our society thinks that we are so deserving that we can't even follow our own rules or laws, let alone those in the Bible. How many times have you seen a car parked out front of the Dry Cleaners, in the red curb zone? How many times does a car pass you on the right side in the service lane to get ahead in traffic? How many times do parents tell school officials that their child can't be held accountable? Why do we think that we are so much more important than anyone, or everyone, else?

Serving another is done humbly, out of love, putting them above yourself.

From 2:5, Paul writes: "Your attitude should be the same as that of Christ Jesus..." The attitudes he lists include:

- He did not promote His equality with God, but instead emptied Himself to be in likeness of all men
- He humbled Himself to the point of accepting death, even death on the cross.

From Galatians 5:13-14:

¹³You, my brothers, were called to be free. But do not use your freedom to indulge the sinful nature; rather, serve one another in love. ¹⁴The entire law is summed up in a single command: "Love your neighbor as yourself."

We were provided with freedom of choice. With that choice, choose to serve each other. You do that by loving each other as much as you love yourself.

- Tend to others, they may need to be watered or pruned, just like a plant
- Be there for others, be in attendance at their low points as well as their high points
- Do for others, whether they can for themselves, or not
- What better way to serve than to minister to
- Be patient, wait upon the opportunity, requested or not, to serve others

<u>Exercises</u>

1.   First, measure the level of your humility by answering the
following questions, which come from The Berean
Christian Bible Resources:

A.   Do you respond to rebuke by getting angry or by
giving careful consideration to the rebuke?

ANGRY   CONSIDER

B.   If someone disagrees with your opinion, do you
demonize and slander the person, or do you do you try to
understand their point of view?

SLANDER   UNDERSTAND

C.   Are you generally afraid of what people think of
you? It is not characteristic of Biblical humility for one to
place a high value on other people's opinion of them. The
humble are more concerned about doing what is right than
doing things to make themselves more popular. Thus *"the
righteous are as bold as a lion."* **Proverbs 28:1** Confidence
in God is characteristic of Biblical humility. *"So do not
throw away your confidence; it will be richly
rewarded."* **Hebrew 10:35**

AFRAID   NOT AFRAID

D.   When you think of leading someone to Christ, do
you tend to replace the "gospel" with your own personal
testimony?

YES   NO

E.   Do you talk more about Christ of the Bible or more about yourself and your own personal experience of Christ?

CHRIST   YOURSELF

F.   Do you tend to pray more for yourself or more for others?

OTHERS   YOURSELF

G.   Are you involved in regularly meeting the practical needs of others?

YES   NO

H.   Concerning your secular career and ministry objective, are you trying to make something of yourself, or are you trying to make nothing of yourself? (**John 3:30** *"He must become greater; I must become less."*) Is your objective to serve, or simply to make a name for yourself?

SERVE   SELF SERVE

2.   If you find that you are not quite as humble as you thought you might be, develop a plan to make God greater and you less. This plan should include the intention of including biblical stories in your conversations. You should read and have memorized summaries of several stories that will enable you to better discuss your faith and relationship to God.

_____

_____

_____

3.   Find a place to volunteer to be of service to those in need.

_____

_____

_____

Empathize

- Identify with
- Understanding of another's situation
- Relate to
- Feel for
- Feel at one with
- To be sensitive to
- Associate with

When I was in college, I took a couple of Psychology classes under the heading, Interpersonal Relationships. Basically, this was a lesson that originates in empathy. We received quite a bit of training in how to converse with another person in order to help them express what bothers them. Nonverbal communication is important: maintaining eye contact without staring, body posture showing attention instead of boredom, and such. Intent listening was also extremely important. In that line, your responses to the other person were critical. To start, your responses might be nothing more than parroting key phrases back to the other person. When they hear their own thoughts, it prompts them to go deeper, to explain more. Patiently, as you listen more and more, repeating key phrases, you start to add some of your own thoughts through clarifying questions. You try to lead the person ahead to better see the completion of their thoughts or feelings. You must be careful not to impose your beliefs but to represent the other person's.

That training has served me well over the years. Empathy is the ability to get on the same level, to be in the same place, on the same side of the coin, with another person. Gone are your feelings or your perspective of the situation. You try to live and breathe in the space as the other person. Humility remains a part of this. But really, it is the loss of self, the ability to encompass yourself in the reality, or perceptions, of the other person. It is really an emotional connection more than an intellectual one.

The act of living, even in the best of times, contains struggles. What each person deals with is quite different, quite personal. Jesus is asking us to take on the struggles of others, to see and feel as they do, so that we might better minister to them.

Look to the story of The Death and Resurrection of Lazarus in John 11, especially verses 17-45. Twice in this story, in verse 33 and 35, Jesus is weeping, is deeply moved by the loss that both Mary and Martha feel from the death of their brother, Lazarus. Verse 35 simply says, "Jesus wept." In verse 38, Jesus is once again described as being deeply moved within. Jesus shows empathy, He is able to shake off His identity and relate on a very personal level with Mary and Martha, literally feeling their pain.

Now look to Luke 17:1-4, verse 4 being:

> [4]"If he sins against you seven times in a day, and seven times comes back to you and says, 'I repent,' forgive him."

This would be quite a difficult challenge. If someone were to sin against you seven times in a day, and all seven times honestly and sincerely repent to you, Jesus is asking that you forgive them. In order to do this you would really have to understand their motivation and their shame. It would be extremely difficult to leave behind the hurt or harm that this person has caused you to feel what they feel, to see from their point of view. But this, God asks of us.

If you are able to remove the act of judgment from your behavior, that would be a big step towards empathy. In this case it would be so easy to judge this person, thinking them a liar, a coward trying to avoid responsibility. But it is not our right to judge another person as God would. Go back to the story of Lazarus in John 11:

> [33]When Jesus saw her weeping, and the Jews who had come along with her also weeping, he was deeply moved in spirit and troubled. [34]"Where have you laid him?" he asked.

"Come and see, Lord," they replied.

[35]Jesus wept.

[36]Then the Jews said, "See how he loved him!"

[37]But some of them said, "Could not he who opened the eyes of the blind man have kept this man from dying?"

In verse 37 you can see, that we as humans find it extremely difficult to stop judging others. Here one of them can't help but say, perhaps sarcastically, "Why didn't Jesus just save him from dying?"

It is not for us to judge the path that God has chosen. God chose to use the death of Lazarus as a time for Jesus to be there and for those people in attendance, believers or not, to see the miracle. We do not know what God has planned for anyone in this story. In this case, it was our job to empathize with Mary and Martha; to show them love and compassion. Judgment is not our right and will prevent us from truly empathizing with others. We know not what God has planned; we need only do our best to listen to Him when He presents us with the opportunities to be Christ-like.

A friend of mine told me this story of his son, the star high school football player. At his school, there was a girl, smart, but overweight. In the competitive world of teen-aged girls, being overweight is quite the "sin." Many of the students took to picking on her, calling her names, making fun of her. One day, in the cafeteria, the football star stood up, walked over to the girl's table and sat down with her. When other students came by to make fun of her, he defended her. My friend was so proud, that his son was able to get out of his own skin and walk in the shoes of this girl. This is what empathy looks like.

- Identify with others
- Be understanding of another's situation, get out of your own skin
- Relate to another person by taking the time to learn who they are, what their perception is
- Feel for others, expand your emotions
- Feel at one with the other person, join their struggle
- To be sensitive to all, realize what impact your footprints leave on others
- Associate with individuals, not groups

Exercises

Read the article, "Have a Heart: The Empathy Workout" by Martha Beck in the March 2006 edition of O Magazine, that can be found at this link:

http://www.oprah.com/article/omagazine/ss_omag_200603_mbeck/1

1. For one week, once a day, do Exercise #1 from the article.

2. For one week, once a day, do Exercise #2 from the article.

3. For one week, once a day, do Exercise #3 from the article.

4. Do some research on line, or in the library, on learning empathetic listening skills.

Present

- To introduce
- To make a gift of
- To offer for observation
- To show or display
- To make known
- Acquaint

About once a week I go to this McDonalds close to my office for lunch. In the short time that it takes to place my order, this particular cashier welcomes me by calling me "Darlin'" (I live in Atlanta), lets me know that she is blessed by God, and asks God to also bless me. She does this with most every customer that comes in. It is still so genuine in her presentation that it just gives you that good feeling as you walk to your table with a burger and fries. What a wonderful way to present God.

This next step in being Christ-like is to introduce God to people, to situations where He has not yet been made aware to those involved. As a Christian we believe that God is omnipresent. Since that is a very difficult concept to grasp, we often forget that He is with us in everything we do. Non-Christians will really have no idea that God is present in their lives. It is our responsibility to move one step further from acting like a good Christian to actually, verbally or visually, asking God to become involved.

In a restaurant, you have seen people saying a blessing before they eat. They are making a visual representation for others to see of inviting God into that moment. Have you ever started a planning session with your colleagues with the phrase, "If it is in God's will...?"

As you expand your world, start meeting people outside of your comfort zone, you will run into people or places where it appears that no one knows God. This is when you need to present Him. Conducting yourself in Christ-like behavior is a good start. However, you may be called upon to relate a personal story of how God influenced your life in a similar circumstance. You might recall a favorite Bible story or passage and share it. You need to be prepared to explain your faith, for people will ask you. I like the thought of making a gift, or a present, of God. Get to the point whereby you fully understand the situation you are in and then, wrap a story of God with personal experience and give it to those in need. Bring up God, talk about your faith, in your conversations with friends and acquaintances. When people come to you for advice, include God as the solution.

Now, look to the story of Paul at Thessalonica in Acts 17. Paul is a persistent presenter of God, first in verses 2-4:

> [2]As his custom was, Paul went into the synagogue, and on three Sabbath days he reasoned with them from the Scriptures, [3]explaining and proving that the Christ had to suffer and rise from the dead. "This Jesus I am proclaiming to you is the Christ," he said. [4]Some of the Jews were persuaded and joined Paul and Silas, as did a large number of God-fearing Greeks and not a few prominent women.

Next, in verses 10-12:

> [10]As soon as it was night, the brothers sent Paul and Silas away to Berea. On arriving there, they went to the Jewish synagogue. [11]Now the Bereans were of more noble character than the Thessalonians, for they received the message with great eagerness and examined the Scriptures every day to see if what Paul said was true. [12]Many of the Jews believed, as did also a number of prominent Greek women and many Greek men.

And again, in 16-20:

[16]While Paul was waiting for them in Athens, he was greatly distressed to see that the city was full of idols. [17]So he reasoned in the synagogue with the Jews and the God-fearing Greeks, as well as in the marketplace day by day with those who happened to be there. [18]A group of Epicurean and Stoic philosophers began to dispute with him. Some of them asked, "What is this babbler trying to say?" Others remarked, "He seems to be advocating foreign gods." They said this because Paul was preaching the good news about Jesus and the resurrection. [19]Then they took him and brought him to a meeting of the Areopagus, where they said to him, "May we know what this new teaching is that you are presenting? [20]You are bringing some strange ideas to our ears, and we want to know what they mean."

I would like to add verse 34 as well to illustrate a point:

[34]A few men became followers of Paul and believed. Among them was Dionysius, a member of the Areopagus, also a woman named Damaris, and a number of others.

Three times in this story, and in three different places, Paul introduces God to groups of people. Even though he got into quite a bit of trouble in doing so, he persevered. In today's society, the chance of being locked up for speaking of God is slim. However, we might experience negative peer pressure, or snickers, or gossip. We can't let this stop us. Search for places where God is missing, where people are in need of Him, and present Him.

Each of the passages above contains another interesting piece. In each instance, Paul was able to get people interested in God, some to the point of becoming followers, believers. It is not our job to measure the success of the times in which we present God. However, be comforted in knowing, that you will have an effect on the people you present to. You probably won't see the effect, but know that people will leave that encounter with you with the seed of God planted in them. And from that seed, God will take over.

- Introduce God to your friends, to people that don't know Him
- Make a gift of God by wrapping Him in a personal story
- Put God forward into situations where a solution is needed, and let Him be evaluated
- Show God's love by displaying it to others
- Let people know that you are a believer, that God is in your heart
- Make God a part of your conversations so that, at the very least, He is an acquaintance to those in your life

Exercises

For this exercise, you are to find biblical stories that you can memorize summaries of. In essence, you would like to find stories that will enable you to relate better to the questions from people that do not have God in their lives. You will need to anticipate some of the topics ahead of time, which might include faith, love, service, etc. And, over time and experience, you should add to your mental library of stories when new topics are presented to you.

You might find some of the on-line Bible research sites to be of use. For example, www.BibleGateway.com provides a topical index you can use to locate stories based on key words like those provided above.

List some of the types of questions you might receive from non-believers, and then the corresponding story/verse you will memorize in preparation for those questions.

_____

_____

_____

_____

_____

_____

Involve

Involve God in your plans

- To include
- To have as a necessary feature
- To engage
- To connect closely
- To influence
- To wrap or envelop
- To subsume

Have you ever been "in the zone?" If you are an athlete, or have watched any championship sporting event, you know what this means. When you are in the zone, you feel that you can do nothing wrong. The basket is bigger. The bat swings harder. The ball flies further. The pass is more accurate. You just can't miss. These feelings, for most of us are few and far between. But when you're in it, it is a special time!

In a later chapter, I will discuss how I believe God speaks in opportunities, and that there are opportunities in every moment of every day. If you can believe that, you can literally be speaking with God almost constantly. What a special feeling that is?

God offers us opportunities to be Christ-like in every moment. If we are aware of these choices, we find ourselves talking to God more frequently. Some of the opportunities we face meet us with easy decisions of following the lead of Jesus. Other opportunities present choices that will be more difficult to understand, or might be far more difficult to live up to than we think we can handle at that time. When these arise, I find myself talking with God more and more. And, when I make the correct choice, and God shows me the fruits of that choice, I feel fantastic. When the good choices I make have a positive impact in the world around me, I can't help but feel like I can't miss, that I am in the zone. And this zone is really the place to be.

You should invite God to be involved in your personal plans. In addition, as you meet with people, and they need God in their lives, you need to actively involve God in your discussions with them. Once you are in the habit of including God in your plans, He becomes a necessary component of your living. Having that relationship will permeate into other relationships with other people. When they can see how closely you are connected to God, and how you are at peace with your place in life, they can experience the calm that you offer. They can feel God through you.

Look to the stories, "Jesus Feeds the Five Thousand" and "Jesus Walks on Water," in Matthew 14. First, Jesus was able to feed the multitude with five loaves of bread and two fish. He did this by blessing the food and involving God in His plan. And at the end of these stories, in Gennesaret, people went far and wide to bring the sick to Jesus to be healed. They were healed by simply touching the fringe of His cloak. They reached out to touch Jesus, to be engaged with Him, to connect to Him.

To me, the interesting part is in the middle of these stories.

> [25]During the fourth watch of the night Jesus went out to them, walking on the lake. [26]When the disciples saw him walking on the lake, they were terrified. "It's a ghost," they said, and cried out in fear.

> [27]But Jesus immediately said to them: "Take courage! It is I. Don't be afraid."

> [28]"Lord, if it's you," Peter replied, "tell me to come to you on the water."

> [29]"Come," he said.

Then Peter got down out of the boat, walked on the water and came toward Jesus. [30]But when he saw the wind, he was afraid and, beginning to sink, cried out, "Lord, save me!"

[31]Immediately Jesus reached out his hand and caught him. "You of little faith," he said, "why did you doubt?"

[32]And when they climbed into the boat, the wind died down. [33]Then those who were in the boat worshiped him, saying, "Truly you are the Son of God."

The disciples were out on the boat, in the middle of the night, during a bad storm. They must have had misgivings about the trouble they were in. Jesus must have understood their dilemma and came to them. At first they didn't recognize Him. Then, Jesus invited Peter to walk out on the water to Him. As long as Peter was connected to Jesus, enveloped in his belief, he was fine. As soon as he became distracted, moved away from Jesus in his mind, he began to sink. And, when they all got back on board, and the disciples again recognized Jesus as the Son of God, the winds died down.

We must believe in God. We must not doubt. We must involve Him in our lives, in our plans. By maintaining that bond with God, others will come to enjoy the same relationship, the same love from God.

- Include God in your plans, and the plans you help others to make
- God must be a necessary part of your life, and visible to others
- Remain engaged with God in every moment that you can
- Be closely connected to God and include others in your circle

- Allow God's influence on you to be displayed to those around you
- Wrap yourself in the love of God
- Christ-like behavior must be the basic, general rule in your life; let Him subsume you

Exercises

1. Get yourself involved. Find a new group, whether it be a Bible study group or a volunteer organization. What new groups should you investigate?

    _____

    _____

    _____

2. Prepare to listen to all of the people in your world. Be tuned to hear when situations arise with people that do not have God involved. If you are not able to involve God at that time, go home, pray about what to say, look up some passages in the Bible that might relate, and then make the plan to go back to that person prepared to involve God in your discussion. What stories might you need to read to be prepared?

    _____

    _____

    _____

Save

- To rescue from harm
- To redeem
- To set free from the consequences of sin
- To prevent the waste or loss of
- To treat with care
- To deliver from misery or evil
- To extricate from danger

Now we come to the top of the hierarchy. So far, as we have covered Pursue, Serve, Empathize, Present, and, Involve, most any person could feel that these are tasks that can be done. As a human being, we are capable of accomplishing those goals. But when we discuss the act of Saving a soul, most of us will stop and think that there is no way that we can save any soul. And, in fact, we can't.

A simple prayer that I say frequently is, "Lord, let me be the conduit through which the light of Your love shines through."

We cannot make the assumption that we are empowered to save a soul. If we were to place that possibility in our minds, we would be continually frustrated because we wouldn't be able to achieve it. However, if we believe that through us God will save souls; that is something completely different. That is attainable. And, that is very rewarding.

Our influence on people that we try to bring to Jesus follows the same path of that of a teacher. Our amount of involvement in the relationship with that person through the first five levels, Pursue, Serve, Empathize, Present, and, Involve, is quite high. We are also trying to create an environment of discovery for that person. Discovery being that God is present and is waiting for an invitation to be a recognizably active part of their life. But when that person comes to the level of being Saved, our role needs to diminish and let that person, with his own thinking and his own relationship with God, move forward.

Look to the two stories in Mark 5. The first is the story of Jesus healing the Gerasene Demonaic. In this story a man comes to Jesus asking not to be tormented by Him. Instead, Jesus asks his name and finds that he is possessed by Legion. Through the man's belief in Jesus, and His love for the man, God removes the legion and the man is saved, going home to proclaim all that Jesus has done for him.

In the second story, as Jesus comes ashore, Jairus, an official of the synagogue, tells Jesus of his dying daughter. As Jesus is walking through the masses of people to see the daughter, He is touched by an ill woman, who is cured through her belief in Him. By the time Jesus got to the house of the dying girl, He was told that she had died. Jesus stated that she was just sleeping, and as He moved to go see her, several of the people began to laugh at Him. However, Jesus awoke the girl.

Both of these stories show the power of God and His ability to save souls. These stories are reference to us displaying the soul saving ability of belief in God.

The second story has two interesting side plots. First, the ill woman, believing that simply touching Jesus will heal her, touches his garments. And then,

> [30]At once Jesus realized that power had gone out from him. He turned around in the crowd and asked, "Who touched my clothes?"
>
> [31]"You see the people crowding against you," his disciples answered, "and yet you can ask, 'Who touched me?' "
>
> [32]But Jesus kept looking around to see who had done it. [33]Then the woman, knowing what had happened to her,

came and fell at his feet and, trembling with fear, told him the whole truth. [34]He said to her, "Daughter, your faith has healed you. Go in peace and be freed from your suffering."

The act of the woman expressing her belief in Jesus, the act of touching His clothes, made an impact on Jesus. Even with the mass of people jostling around Him, He felt the act of belief from one individual.

Second, Jesus is told that the dying girl has in fact passed;

[38]When they came to the home of the synagogue ruler, Jesus saw a commotion, with people crying and wailing loudly. [39]He went in and said to them, "Why all this commotion and wailing? The child is not dead but asleep." [40]But they laughed at him.

After he put them all out, he took the child's father and mother and the disciples who were with him, and went in where the child was.

Jesus was laughed at because of His faith. We need to understand that many times other people will not understand our faith and the power that it holds. We must not be swayed or detoured from the path our faith leads us. Jesus paid no mind to those that were laughing, instead, He continued with His faith which brought the girl back from the dead.

Now, look to the story of Philip and the Ethiopian in Acts 8:25-40. This is a story of how God will use us as the conduit to save souls.

Philip is called to Pursue:

[29]The Spirit told Philip, "Go to that chariot and stay near it."

Philip Serves and Empathizes:

³⁰Then Philip ran up to the chariot and heard the man reading Isaiah the prophet. "Do you understand what you are reading?" Philip asked.

³¹"How can I," he said, "unless someone explains it to me?" So he invited Philip to come up and sit with him.

Philip Presents and Involves God:

³⁴The eunuch asked Philip, "Tell me, please, who is the prophet talking about, himself or someone else?" ³⁵Then Philip began with that very passage of Scripture and told him the good news about Jesus.

Philip Saves:

³⁶As they traveled along the road, they came to some water and the eunuch said, "Look, here is water. Why shouldn't I be baptized?" ³⁸And he gave orders to stop the chariot. Then both Philip and the eunuch went down into the water and Philip baptized him.

Not all of us can baptize another person, but we can lead them to the water.

- Rescue others from the harm they will endure in a life without Christ
- Redeem, restore the honor of other's souls
- Set others free from the consequences of sin
- Prevent the waste or loss of another soul
- Treat with care
- Deliver other people from misery or evil
- Extricate others from danger by bringing God into their lives

✦ ✦ ✦

<u>Exercises</u>

Read the blog at the following site:

http://www.revelife.com/Revelife/693367969/advice-how-do-you-start-a-conversation-about-god-with-a-non-believer/?ref=xn

Choose one person in your world that appears not to have God in their life. Spend time with them and get to know them better. Prepare your response for when they first ask you about God in your life.

_____

_____

_____

Your Walk

I was born and raised Catholic. I have to say that my attempt at being Catholic ended in my teenage years and that I went for another twenty years or so with little to no faith. My wife is Baptist and we agreed to raise our children in the Baptist church. As I started attending church and Sunday School classes, my re-introduction to God began. One thing that I learned, different from when I was younger, was that God is approachable. I was impressed that I was surrounded by people that believed that they could have a one on one relationship with God. This was new to me.

I fought my involvement with church for quite awhile, and remained in a self-destructive mode for a long time. Fortunately, my wife stayed with me. Then, one day, God spoke with me, and I with Him, and my life has changed dramatically since then. At that point, when I sat in Sunday School classes, I realized that while many of those around me believed that they could speak directly with God, they questioned whether they really had or not. They prayed, and thought that God heard their prayers. But, they were waiting for an audible word from God, or a visual sign. They felt remorse in that they were still waiting for evidence of direct communication with Him.

About this time I began to see that God speaks in many ways. One of those ways is in opportunities. God presents us with opportunities in which we can decide how we can most follow His path and be Christ-like, or, deviate from that path and follow our own agenda, our own flesh. And, when you believe that this is in fact a method of communicating with God, and that there is an opportunity in every moment of every day, you can see that you can speak with God as often as you like, and He talks back.

I also recognized that my state of faith, of believing, of being a member of a church, was very immature. I was very naive. I didn't know much scripture. I didn't know all of the bible stories that teachers kept referencing. I felt at a loss when it came time to discuss faith and religious issues. So, I decided to write a Sunday School curriculum. I titled it, "Your Walk," and my church has been gracious enough to let me teach it to several classes. One of the first things I tell each new class is that I wrote this curriculum for very selfish reasons; that I wanted to learn from my students. To this day, and probably unfortunately for my students, I still learn more from them than they learn from me.

As stated, our goal on earth is to live a human life as close to Christ-like as we possibly can. God has offered us a path for our life. In a very personal way, we interact with God during our walk while we stray from and relocate this path over and over again.

The next few chapters in this book contain some of the lessons from the class, Your Walk. My overall objective is to facilitate the strengthening of the personal relationship between God and you. This class is designed for self-actualization. This means that I have offered readings and exercises that are to be done on your own. The more a student puts into this class, the more they get out of it. For several people, some personal realizations have been quite impactful.

__Exercises__

The term "elevator speech" is used quite frequently in business. It refers to a monologue that one prepares in order to present their concept, or make a sales pitch, in the time it takes to ride an elevator from one floor to another. Of course, if you only go one floor, that speech could be quite short, versus riding an elevator for twenty floors.

Write out an elevator speech that answers the question, "What does it mean to be a Christian?"

You are preparing a speech so that when a non-Christian asks you some questions, you are ready. You could anticipate other questions that might pop up and prepare speeches for them as well. Some examples might be:

- How did you become a follower of God?
- Why do you bring your children to church?
- Describe your relationship with God.

_____

_____

_____

_____

_____

_____

What is Your Legacy?

It is our goal to lead a Christ-like life. What better way to measure that effort than by evaluating the impact that you have left on others? Everybody, when they pass, will leave some form of legacy, the remembrance of that person spoken about by others. As a Christian, we hope that what people say about us will reflect the image of Christ.

There are two ways in which to measure this. The first would be quantitative. We have spoken about expanding your world of influences. If you were to pass and the number of people that remember you and speak of you would be limited to your close family and a couple of friends; that would say one thing. However, if the number of people that remember you also include colleagues and co-workers, students and teachers, other relatives from aunts and uncles and cousins, your postman and your hair dresser, that would say quite something else about your life.

The second measure would be qualitative. Obviously, we want people to speak well of us. However, how will they remember our struggle to be Christ-like? Will they describe your life, your walk on earth, as being close to God? If they had to describe you in a sentence or two, would they include God in their words?

I don't mean to sound morbid, but, thinking about your passing and the impact that it would have on those people in your world can help you make better decisions in the moment by moment of opportunities that God provides us with. If you think of what your spouse, or children might say about a thought, or an action, that you are about to make, that could influence your decision. If you stop to think of what your co-workers will say about you, it might change your direction. If you can remember that God sees everything that you think and do, to stay within His grace you will strive to make better decisions.

Please look to the Parable of the Rich Fool in Luke 12:13-21:

> [13]Someone in the crowd said to him, "Teacher, tell my brother to divide the inheritance with me."
>
> [14]Jesus replied, "Man, who appointed me a judge or an arbiter between you?" [15]Then he said to them, "Watch out! Be on your guard against all kinds of greed; a man's life does not consist in the abundance of his possessions."
>
> [16]And he told them this parable: "The ground of a certain rich man produced a good crop. [17]He thought to himself, 'What shall I do? I have no place to store my crops.'
>
> [18]"Then he said, 'This is what I'll do. I will tear down my barns and build bigger ones, and there I will store all my grain and my goods. [19]And I'll say to myself, "You have plenty of good things laid up for many years. Take life easy; eat, drink and be merry." '
>
> [20]"But God said to him, 'You fool! This very night your life will be demanded from you. Then who will get what you have prepared for yourself?'
>
> [21]"This is how it will be with anyone who stores up things for himself but is not rich toward God."

God wants us to understand that our profession, the act of "making a living," is not all that we were put on earth to do. Our profession need not make us who we are. We need to put forth great effort outside of our professions to lead a Christ-like life, to have an impact in our communities and our expanded world. And in so doing, we need to store up our good deeds in the memories of others. We are not to strive towards accumulating wealth for ourselves. Instead, we are to serve and attend to others, creating deposits of Christ-like memories for others to share. It will be the residual impact upon other people by which God will measure the worth of our souls.

Finally, we need to remember that we can be taken from this life at any moment. We really don't have the luxury to keep on-going feuds with family members or friends. We can't simply think that we are in a poor mood and therefore don't have to be nice to that co-worker or waiter or anyone else stuck in the same traffic jam. Living a Christ-like life means that you must act like Christ in every moment. It can't simply be an attitude that we adopt when we feel like it.

<u>Exercises</u>

1.   (Complete this task before reading the next tasks)
Prepare a list of people in your life. Two or three should be
significant people, those that you love. And, two or three
should be acquaintances, such as your hairdresser/barber, a
colleague at work, the security guard at the office, your
postal worker, etc.

For each person on that list, write down what you believe
they would say about you right now if you were to pass
away.

PEOPLE YOU LOVE

_____

_____

_____

ACQUAINTANCES

_____

_____

_____

2.	Answer this question, "What would you like God to say to you when you meet at the pearly gates?"

	_____

	_____

	_____

3.	Go back to your list from number one above and re-read what those people might have said about you. Do any of their comments describe you as a follower of God, as being Christ-like? If not, why not?

	_____

	_____

	_____

4.	For those people on your list that did not perceive you as being Christian, make a plan to show them that you are. Then, act on it.

5.	Listen to the song "Live Like You're Dying" by Tim McGraw.

Color Your Soul

This is perhaps my favorite lesson in the curriculum. The thought is based on a poem I wrote some twenty-six years ago, when, as a non-believer, I attempted to describe the procession of a person's soul from birth to heaven. In my poem, I used the word "Spirit" for "Soul." Here is that poem:

Spirit

Birth

It was luminous and shaped but shapeless
It arrayed in angular hues from the coldest of cold to the hottest of hot, but it did not threaten
It floated but looked as if it had weight, substance
It would move, slow and darting, but at length the whole appeared immobile
"Why?" I asked of it and it flickered
I pondered and so did it

Through many days we learned a language, but not one of mouth, and ideas flowed as the ceaseless waves
I learned of it
I became frightened to believe; to believe that I must leave
Accept...accepted
Engulf...engulfed
Share, shared, sharing
We
We did and became
Life was me and I was alive

Life

Cry, and breathe a strange air

Be cold and hungry
Intellect hidden behind years
Luminous behind my eyes but not seen; forgotten until death
But alive now...What?
"Why?" I asked of it and it eluded and was gone
Warmth and nourishment; body, senses, growth
Fulfill, enjoy, overwhelm, power, movement, lasting
I am here

Man, Love...loving
Breathe...breathing
Child to adolescent, adolescent to adult
I grow, live and experience
Living, the luminescence is not seen
Some kneel to it but I seek the light in life, living and loving
It remains elusive but chasing enlightens both of us
Growing and learning, knowing and lacking, having and wanting;
these, the roads my path follows
Conflict and serenity

Death

Sleep
Eyes closed, luminous appears
Hues slower, weight heavier, bright mellower
I am no longer, it seems aged
"Why?" I ask of it and it departed; yeah and me with it
We, as one again, fly on wingless abandon to an airless moon

Wind rushes past displaying my life
I relive through an extra consciousness of perception
Time and learning travel hand in hand afore me
Wind ceases and I fly to a haven of lights
Lights of different hues from me
I remain I, but become many to spend time

This old poem of mine has yielded an analogy that I use for this lesson. All of us are born with a soul. At birth that soul is like a pure white, amorphous gas cloud. The white represents love, and the pure white is the love of God. As we go through life, we begin to add colors. Red could represent anger; green jealousy; blue bitterness, and so on. So that when we die, our souls are a mix of color wisps interspersed through our cloud. Each of us has a unique soul. And, when we get to heaven, we get to share our souls with every other soul there. We are able to experience all of the colors that make up the souls of others, and through time we learn from us all.

Every experience we have while living leaves an unforgettable mark, or color, on our soul. You might read the following passages from the Bible that will provide qualities, both positive and negative, that are worthy of assigning colors as they become part of your soul:

> Galatians 5:16-26   Colossians 3:12
> 1 Timothy 6:11   Ephesians 4:32
> 1 Peter 2:1   1 Peter 3:8

In the class I teach, as in the Exercise section of this book, I give an assignment to literally color your soul. The following picture is what I drew to display my soul. Following it is a brief narrative describing the nuances of my soul. Unfortunately, in this book, this picture is in black and white.

NARRATIVE:

Here is a picture of my soul. At birth it was pure white with the love of God. However, as I have lived I have put colors into it. Love is white, and hate is black. Kindness is yellow while bitterness is blue. Forgiveness is red and jealousy is green. Some of the stories making up my soul include:

In the lower right hand corner, there is a black spot. I had a roommate in college that stole a championship ring my grandfather left to me when he passed. I was full of hate and wanted badly to hurt him when I found out that he pawned it off for a few bucks. I never got it back.

In the real picture within a flare of yellow is a white spot. When my daughter was learning to walk, we lived in a townhouse with three levels and many sets of staircases. My daughter walked to the top of a staircase and before I could grab her, tottered off. I dove after her, catching her to my chest, wrapped her in my arms and together, we went bumping down the steps on my back. That was when I learned what unconditional love was.

Again, in the real picture, off to the bottom is a small smudge of green. I was laid off of my job back in the early 90's. I started my own consulting company. For a long time it was a struggle to make ends meet. My best friend and neighbor had a very good job. He was able to skip out and play golf, go drinking with his buddies, pretty much whatever he wanted and still brought home a good paycheck. I was full of jealousy.

Fortunately, I have been very happily married now for more than twenty years. That is not to say that at times I haven't had my difficulties in maintaining a positive outlook on our relationship. A long time ago I used to keep score, meaning that if my wife got to do something or buy something, then I felt that I deserved something just as valuable as well. In addition, if I felt that she did something against me, like a misplaced comment or forgot to do something I asked for, I would let it fester inside me. Finally, I was able to forgive her of all of the implications I placed on her. The act of forgiveness, surrounding love, is a red flare with white in the middle.

✧ ✧ ✧

In one of the classes I taught, I had a real artist as a member. She created the picture you see on the cover of this book. What a beautiful picture! Read how beautiful her soul is:

I thank God for the opportunity to do an art therapy project that depicts my immortal soul. The media is transparent glass paint found at a craft store. The surface is a large clear acrylic sheet framed in black--the sin that completely surrounds my soul. In the center is a pure white space that represents my soul's purity, when I was born. The sections around the center are pastel in value because, as a baby, my soul reflected the beginning of emotions, but they were faint and still washed with purity. The vertical "elevator" colors on both sides of my white soul block are the key emotions that developed as I grew- green for envy, blue for passion, yellow for creativity and red for love.

I chose a design with 4 quadrants to reflect the emotions and people in the 4 main categories of my life; childhood, marriage, career, and spiritual. The design also has several sides to each compartment. I typically FEEL several emotions at the same time and it isn't often possible to pin them down with just one color. Also there is the underlying color in each section. For instance in the Career area, the underlying color is Yellow, which is the color for creativity. The colors also represent people in my life in some quadrants, and emotions in others. For instance the royal blue in my childhood is my dad, and in the other 3 quadrants, blue represents "hard work".

The lower right quadrant is my childhood. This is where my inner conflicts began to erupt. I realized that the underlying emotion of my childhood was envy (green). I was firstborn and always expected to be perfect. I was smart enough, but heavier than my parents would have liked. It was always something we fought about. My younger sisters were skinny, and that set me up for some very unhappy thoughts. I realize that there was some love (red) and lots of good girlie vibes (pink) and a lot of creative talent passed down (yellow), but love was minimal in that quadrant.

The lower left section is my career. I soon learned that my hard work (blue) and my creativity (yellow) were a magic combination in my work environment. Additionally, I could SELL (gold glitter) and made it all profitable. I was lucky enough to be chosen for some TV selling work which was glamorous (silver glitter). And underlying it all was my love of productive work AND productive leisure. It served me well.

The upper left area is my married life and family. There was much love (red) in the beginning and passion (blue + red makes purple). However, soon, too soon, after the wedding, an addiction (dark gray) took center stage. It was underneath everything--even after the divorce, addiction controlled us. But then my daughter found a wonderful man (Lt. Blue Sparkle) and he allowed us to stop taking ourselves so seriously (Clear Sparkle for laughter). I'm glad to say that we are a very small, very loving family with lots of Girlie vibes (pinks) and that love has definitely won out over the addiction.

The upper right section is my relationship with God. Notice that all the emotions exist, but He has paid the price and sanctified them, therefore they are all still there, but they sparkle. And the underlying color is red for love--not only my love for Him, but especially His love for me. He has blessed my family in all ways. There is financial blessing (gold glitter) and satisfying work (blue glitter) and success (silver glitter) and yes, He has even sanctified the envy (green glitter) into an earnest desire to keep my weight down and my body healthy.

The sides of the geometric design tie the quadrants together and signify the love of God for me throughout my life. The divine sparkle has kept me from giving in to my emotions and allowed me to keep going forward to better times and new opportunities to serve HIM. Thank you, God, for my immortal soul and the chance to be washed with your love, so that my soul will be white and pure again--in the hereafter.

✧ ✧ ✧

Exercises

Get a piece of paper and some crayons, or a canvas and some paint, or whatever other medium you would like to work with and, color your soul. First, think hard about all of the experiences in your life that have left a mark on your soul and determine which ones you want to display, and how. Every color, every stroke, should have meaning from your life.

You might consider some of the following passages to help you remember the types of marks that impact your soul:

- Galatians 5:16-26
- Colossians 3:12
- 1 Timothy 6:11
- Ephesians 4:32
- 1 Peter 2:1, 3:8

Our Goal is to be Christ-like

I have to admit that, to the chagrin of my wife, I'm a Sci-Fi fan. If you are too, you may be interested in this analogy.

In the TV show, Star Trek Next Generation, there is a character named Data. Data is an android, devoid of any human emotions. He is a perfect machine but has evolved to a point that he understands how different from humans he is and it bothers him. There is an episode titled, "The Offspring" in which Data creates a daughter. He has worked hard at incorporating human emotions into his daughter, to the point that the emotions conflict with the computer processing and she begins to fail. Data works as hard as he possibly can but cannot save his daughter. His colleagues, at the end of his loss, ask him, "Data you are the perfect being. You have all of the processing capabilities of the best computers; you have the strength of ten humans. But, you keep trying to become more like us, to become human. Why?"

Data's response, "It is the struggle to be human that matters; that is what I will be measured by."

We are made in God's image. We are very close to perfect, perhaps superior to every other creature God has created. But our goal is to become as much like Christ as we possibly can. None of us will ever become Christ. However, it is the struggle to become like Christ that matters; that is what we will be measured by.

Look to the story where Samuel anoints David in 1 Samuel 16:1-13. Then, re-read verse 7:

> But the LORD said to Samuel, "Do not consider his appearance or his height, for I have rejected him. The LORD does not look at the things man looks at. Man looks at the outward appearance, but the LORD looks at the heart."

How does our culture define success? Many of us might consider a person with the latest fashions, or the newest car, or the biggest house, to be successful. Are possessions the measure of our success? In the passage above, God says no. He measures the heart. He measures our intent. He measures our awareness of His wishes and then our delivery on making them happen.

In the Exercise section that relates to this chapter, there are quite a few passages to read that show us examples of Christ-like behavior. I would like to present a couple of my favorites here as well.

From Colossians 3:14

> And over all these virtues put on love, which binds them all together in perfect unity.

The picture of waking up in the morning and spiritually putting on a cloak of love pops into my head every time I read this passage. As we go out to face the world, imagine that we are able to put on love and take that attitude with us as we meet each and everybody that day.

From Galatians 5:13

> You, my brothers, were called to be free. But do not use your freedom to indulge the sinful nature; rather, serve one another in love.

Here we are told not to turn the freedom of choice that God has given us into opportunities of the flesh. Instead, use our choice to serve others because we opt to love them.

Philippians 4:5

> Let your gentleness be evident to all. The Lord is near.

Another interpretation of this, "Let your forbearing spirit be known to all men."

1 Peter 2:20

> But how is it to your credit if you receive a beating for doing wrong and endure it? But if you suffer for doing good and you endure it, this is commendable before God.

Another interpretation, "If doing right you still suffer for it, endure it with patience." This has always been a tough concept for me. There are times when we might feel like we are performing good deeds and treating others well for a long stretch of time, but if we are expecting something in return for that, we probably should be thinking something else. There will not necessarily be any reward on this earth for doing good deeds out of love for others. In fact, we might suffer for it. This passage tells us to endure the suffering and that God will reward us for those efforts in heaven.

Look to Matthew 6:1-18. This passage covers charity, prayer and fasting. For each, Jesus is telling us not to do any of these three acts in a display for others. We are to perform these acts out of love, not for an expectation of praise, reward or recognition from other people. Put love in your heart, mind and actions; and, quietly, humbly, go about your business.

✧ ✧ ✧

Exercises

The Bible offers many ways in which we can live our life like Jesus did. Read through the following verses until you find one that poses a challenge for you. When you find it, read it through several times. Recall the experiences in your life where this behavior has been difficult for you to portray. Pray for the people that might have been affected by your behavior. Pray that God might give you more opportunities to improve in that area.

James 1:19	I Corinthians 16:14
Matthew 5:25	Philippians 4:5
Colossians 3:14	I Peter 5:5
Galatians 6:2	I Peter 2:20
Galatians 5:13	I Timothy 6:18
Ephesians 4:2	I Thessalonians 5:14
Luke 6:31	

Who are you praying for, and what is your prayer?

_____

_____

_____

_____

_____

Listen to the song "I Can Only Imagine" by MercyMe.

God Speaks in Opportunities

Hopefully you can remember some of that elementary school math from way back when. The > symbol means greater than. The < symbol means less than, and the = symbol means equal. Now that we have that down, let's move on up to high school math and work on a proof. We want to develop an If/Then statement. So, what symbol would you place between these two words?

If,   SIN _____   sin,

As humans, we frequently judge the weight of our sins by the damage that they cause. A "white lie" is less than a real lie. Theft is less than kidnapping which is less than murder. However, if we define sin as the act of moving away from God, then all sin is equal. There is no sin bigger than another. What symbol goes between these two words?

Then,   LOVE _____   love.

(If sin separates us from God, then love brings us closer to God)

If big sin is equal to little sin, then big love is equal to little love. Many times God presents us with opportunities to show our love, and in some of those times we might feel that the amount of our love is insignificant, would have no impact on the situation, and therefore we don't give it. God is not asking us to measure the impact of our love and then decide if we should give it or not. God is simply asking us to love. Love with what you have to give.

I mention the act of giving to beggars on the streets frequently in my classes. More than once, I have had someone say something similar to this: "I saw this guy begging for money. He told me that he hadn't eaten and would use the money to buy food. I told him to meet me at that fast food place across the street and I would bring out a burger and fries for him. He told me that he didn't want that, he just wanted my money. I know he was going to use that money to buy more booze or drugs. I'm not going to give those kinds of people any money."

God asks us to love others as we would love Him. In this case, this beggar is not only asking for money, he is really asking for love. God is presenting us with an opportunity to serve and love another human being. It is not love if we are to put our own conditions on how our charity is to be received. What that person does with our love is between them and God. God will deliver our present of love in the best way for that person to receive it. We simply just need to love that person as we would God.

Read the book of Esther. It is quite an interesting story. In essence, Esther found herself queen to King Xerxes, living in the citadel of Susa. Unknown to the palace and the king, Esther was a Jew, niece to Mordecai. At one point, the second in command to Xerxes, Haman, proposed that all Jews be eliminated and obtained approval from the king. Esther was panicked and didn't know if she should reveal herself to the king, try to hide, or step up to save her people. In Esther 4:14, Mordecai tells her:

> "For if you remain silent at this time, relief and deliverance for the Jews will arise from another place, but you and your father's family will perish. And who knows but that you have come to royal position for such a time as this?"

God presented Esther with an opportunity to save the Jews. She found herself quite conflicted, worrying about her own safety, the safety of her people, the ability to change the mind of her king. Mordecai reminds her that God has put her in this position, that she has attained this position, this experience, so that she might make the best of this opportunity. We, too, need to remember this. God presents us with opportunities, but He has also prepared us to make the best of them. We simply need to have faith in Him.

There is a music video from the band called Nickelback called, "Savin Me." In this video a young man's life is saved by a stranger by stopping him from walking out in front of a bus. From that point on, he can see numbers above people's heads counting backwards. He is able to figure out that these decreasing numbers represent the life span of each person he sees. His goal is to then find the person who's numbers are rapidly approaching zero so that he may save that life.

Now, combining the thought that God speaks in opportunities and that we are to pursue other people to help, this video presents an interesting analogy. We must strive to put ourselves in positions whereby we are actively searching for people to serve, for people to present God to, for people that need to be saved.

In the Exercise portion of this book that relates to this chapter, there are a number of verses to read that could be categorized as answers to opportunities waiting to happen. A few of them include:

From Matthew 5:42:

> Give to the one who asks you, and do not turn away from the one who wants to borrow from you.

This might help you make a decision then next time you are faced with someone begging on the street.

From Ephesians 4:29:

> Do not let any unwholesome talk come out of your mouths, but only what is helpful for building others up according to their needs, that it may benefit those who listen.

Another interpretation of this that I like might read, "Your word should give grace to the moment." If we all were to stop the gossip and instead speak only positively about each other and the situations we find ourselves in, it would be a different world.

Mark 10:43:

> Instead, whoever wants to become great among you must be your servant

We moved to Atlanta when my children were young. On occasion we would go to some of the Atlanta Braves baseball games. Now, I was brought up near Washington DC and grew up basically not looking at the beggars and homeless people on the streets. So, as we walked to and from the stadium, I would ignore those needy people, and steer my family around them so that we didn't have to have any kind of encounter with them. Then, one day, friends of ours asked our son to join them, with a boy the same age, to go to the Braves game. When my son got back, I asked the usual questions like, did he have fun, who won, what was so great about going, etc? My son told me that this really neat thing happened. His story went something like this,

"His dad is really neat. Before we left he must have put a bunch of dollar bills in his pockets 'cause every time we walked by some of those homeless people, he would give us each a dollar to go and put in their cup. That was cool!"

I think that I learned a bigger lesson that day than my son did.

__Exercises__

Watch the movie "Evan Almighty." Pay particular attention to the part in which Evan's wife takes the kids and they are having dinner in a restaurant and God comes and speaks with her. (If you have already seen the movie, this is in Chapter 13 of the movie).

Perform a random act of kindness. Preferably anonymously, regardless of size, just do it.

I like to refer to the following biblical verses as answers to opportunities waiting to happen. Perhaps you might take one a day and include it in your daily devotional.

Philippians 2:3	James 4:11
Ephesians 5:9, 11	I Thessalonians
5:15Ephesians 4:29	Luke 17:4
Hebrews 10:24	Mark 10:43
I Timothy 6:18	Colossians 3:13
2 Corinthians 13:7	Hebrews 12:14
Matthew 5:42	I Peter 2:12
Romans 12:15	Philippians 4:8

The War of Wills

God speaks to us in many ways, one of which is through opportunities. Opportunities need not wait for major events like storms or accidents or prolonged illness or the death of a loved one. If we are in tune with God our openness to see opportunities become far more frequent, literally becoming almost constant. We are faced with the opportunity to be a follower of Christ in every moment of every day, every time we decide what to do next. This is very good news in that through this we can be in contact with God constantly.

The challenge here is a matter of will, His and ours. If we recognize an opportunity that God has put before us and then decide that chance to perform a Christ-like response is not in our best interest, we have put our will ahead of God's. This is the crux of the human condition. God allowed us freedom of choice. And, in being human, there will be many times that we decide on a course that we feel is better for us, choosing not to follow the path that God has put before us. Since we are unable to know what God has planned for the decisions we are asked to make it is very difficult for us to willingly follow His path instead of our own. God does understand this.

Look to Paul's letter to Romans, specifically in Romans 7:14-25. Paul is quite frustrated in not being able to follow the will of God instead of his own will:

> [14]We know that the law is spiritual; but I am unspiritual, sold as a slave to sin. [15]I do not understand what I do. For what I want to do I do not do, but what I hate I do. [16]And if I do what I do not want to do, I agree that the law is good. [17]As it is, it is no longer I myself who do it, but it is sin living in me. [18]I know that nothing good lives in me, that is, in my sinful nature. For I have the desire to do what is good, but I cannot carry it out. [19]For what I do is not the

good I want to do; no, the evil I do not want to do—this I keep on doing. ²⁰Now if I do what I do not want to do, it is no longer I who do it, but it is sin living in me that does it.

²¹So I find this law at work: When I want to do good, evil is right there with me. ²²For in my inner being I delight in God's law; ²³but I see another law at work in the members of my body, waging war against the law of my mind and making me a prisoner of the law of sin at work within my members. ²⁴What a wretched man I am! Who will rescue me from this body of death? ²⁵Thanks be to God—through Jesus Christ our Lord!

So then, I myself in my mind am a slave to God's law, but in the sinful nature a slave to the law of sin.

An illustration of the war of wills might look like the drawing below. From birth, God has chosen a path for us to follow. However, along the way, as opportunities come up, we make decisions based on what we want to do. In those cases we stray from the path. Because we have freedom of choice, God understands this. He simply asks, that when we get to the point that we understand that we have distanced ourselves from Him, that we truly ask forgiveness. Then, God will present us again with opportunities that will enable us to find our way back to the path.

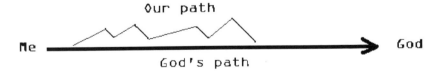

CS Lewis might have summed this up fairly well with the following quote: "The obstacle stopping us from getting closer to God is ourselves, when we can get ourselves out of the way we become more like ourselves, in God's image."

From *Knowing God's Will*, by Winkie Pratney:

"God is looking for willing hearts – those who whole-
heartedly decide to do the will of God. You can know
God's will! God has no favorites. You do not have to be
special, but you have to be available. You do not have to
be clever, but you must be willing to learn from Him. You
do not have to be talented, but you must be willing to obey
whatever He commands. You do not have to possess
much, but you must give everything you have.

God's will for your life is a GOAL, not a blueprint. His
one ultimate goal, or purpose, is for you to be conformed to
the image of His Son, Jesus. God's goal NEVER changes.
A goal is the point you are trying to get to – it sets your
direction. While on your way to this ultimate goal, you
will encounter many smaller goals and purposes along the
way.

Guidance is a lifelong process. God will reveal goals, help
you reach them, then set new, higher ones. Therefore,
knowing God's will for your life is a continued discovery
of the present most effective plan to help you eventually
reach His ultimate goal for you. Should you miss God and
make a wrong decision along the way, all is not lost.
However, many times there are consequences to pay.
Sometimes you may miss an opportunity that may never
again come your way... and many times good years that
belong to God are simply wasted. But the moment our self-
dependence or mistakes are confessed to God, and His
pardon obtained, He will take you where you are at and
work with you, daily pointing out the best course to take in
order for you to reach His ultimate goal for you – to be
conformed to the image of His Son, Jesus."

When you accept that one way God speaks to us is through opportunities, and then agree that these opportunities are in the moments of every day, you are blessed in that you can be in constant dialogue with God. However, this too can be a struggle in that it puts your will in competition with His will over and over again. Don't be overly concerned in the failures to follow His will. Instead, concentrate on the successes you have in hearing His direction, walking on His path. Perhaps Proverbs 16:9 might help:

> [9] In his heart a man plans his course, but the LORD determines his steps.

✦ ✦ ✦

Exercises

1.   Read James 4:13-16. How often have you begun a discussion where you are planning your future with the words, "If it is the Lord's will?" Should this become an integral part in your planning now? Why or why not?

_____

_____

_____

_____

_____

_____

2.   From Vincent van Gogh: "Your profession is not what
        brings home your weekly paycheck; your profession is
        what you're put here on earth to do – with such passion and
        such intensity it becomes a spiritual calling."

        If you truly listened to the Holy Spirit, what would your
        profession be right now? If it is not your current, paid
        profession, what could you do to begin to change?

        _____

        _____

        _____

3.   From Carlo Carretto: "God is always calling us! But there
        are distinctive moments in this call of His, moments which
        leave a permanent mark on us – moments which we never
        forget."

        Recall an example of a permanent mark on your soul from
        God's calling to you.

        _____

        _____

        _____

4.   From Suzanne Farnham: "Circumstance and coincidence may cause us to be in the right place at the right time to do God's work in a specific way."

Recall an example of a time when you were in the right place at the right time.

_____

_____

_____

5.   From William Barry: "A belief that God acts with purpose in this world must lead to attempts, however feeble, to discern how my own actions might be attuned to God's one action."

What has God told you? What do you believe His one action is for you right now? What attempts are you making to work with God?

_____

_____

_____

6.   Listen to "Jesus Take the Wheel" by Carrie Underwood.

7.   Include one of the following verses in your daily
       devotionals:

Romans 12:21   Matthew 26:41
Colossians 3:5   Philippians 2:3
Galatians 5:13   James 4:7
Galatians 6:9   James 1:21, 22
Mark 11:25   Colossians 3:8
Galatians 5:16   Colossians 1:9-10
Colossians 3:15   2 Timothy 2:16
Romans 8:28-29

Related Thoughts

Several years ago I was fortunate enough to be in a Sunday School class in which the instructor gave us an assignment of writing our testimony. He did this from class to class, each class then putting forth a little book. At that point in my life I was really just emerging as a follower of Christ and though quite naïve, my understanding of God was beginning to be formulated. I was lucky in that I took the assignment seriously and wrote a very personal testimony. As part of the assignment, we were to read our testimonies to the class.

I travel frequently, and when doing so reward myself by reading books. Many times I don't know if we've taken off or landed because I get so engrossed in my pleasure reading. The day after I gave my testimony I was to fly off on a business trip somewhere. Once seated, I brought out my paperback and tried to read. However, I was still basking from the light of the day before when God gave me the opportunity to reveal my testimony in public. It was such a wonderful feeling for me that it was all I could think about. I couldn't read. I could only replay that moment in time were I spoke and could see the impact that it had on the people in the audience. I was in the zone!

When you allow yourself to believe that every moment provides you with opportunities from God to speak with Him by your actions, your questions, your thoughts and decisions; you, too, will bask in His light. There is nothing so great as to be in His presence. The simple thing about all of this is that we can be in His presence as often, or as little, as we like.

We discussed the thought of defining your world, not geographically, but socially. Who are the people in your world? And, what can you do to expand your world? Another thought is that the definition of "world" changes with the perspective of the moment. We must be open to flexibility in the boundaries to our world. As God presents us with opportunities in the moments of the day, our world needs to change as those opportunities unfold. Christ had no boundaries to His world; He was able to love everyone as He loved the Father. That is too much for us as humans to fathom. However, as opportunities come before us we must actively search for all of those people involved and then include them in our world of that moment. It is one thing to define our world as family and friends, and then try to expand it by becoming more involved in social circles. This is great in and of itself. However, we must also be able to expand our world in the moments of the day, changing constantly to include those who need to see God through us.

There are two closely related, fun practices that fit within the scope of this book. One is Random Acts of Kindness, the other, Pay It Forward. I went to the movie theater once and the person in front of me paid for my family's tickets. What a wonderful gesture! A random act of kindness. Then, I paid for the next group's tickets, paying it forward. Who knows how long that chain continued, giving good feelings to all that participated? Find ways to perform random acts of kindness, not for recognition, but for the anonymous great feelings you will get as will the receiver of your gift. And, if you are ever in a position of receiving such a gift, pay it forward.

We must establish a relationship with God. Jesus showed us what a personal relationship with God looks like. We must strive to do the same. We must be mutual in our recognition, openness, interests and respect with God. Having a relationship with God will happen through His grace and mercy, but we must be open to it, we must work to keep it going, we must feed it to keep it alive, just like many other relationships. This relationship is built on trust. God is as visible as the wind; you can see the effects if you look. If we hear only silence, it is our own self-imposed silence. Wherever and whenever we seek God, He will meet us there. We should know that being in a relationship with God will be allowing Him to touch us and to change us. He loves us enough to accept us as we are, but He also loves us too much to leave us that way. Expect to be changed, understand that the relationship will mature over time.

In today's world, through various media, the ability to obtain wide ranges of information is done effortlessly. Just turn on the TV or the radio and we are bombarded with good and bad content. There are so many messages in the media today it is nearly impossible to put a filter on them to retain only the good. Many families simply don't allow TV or radio in their homes or cars. Many others try their best to select appropriate shows to watch at home, or, use movie ratings when going to the theaters. But, we all come up short in protecting our children, even ourselves, from receiving content that is not appropriate, that is not reflective of the walk we wish to embody.

Look to I John 4:1-8:

> [1]Dear friends, do not believe every spirit, but test the spirits to see whether they are from God, because many false prophets have gone out into the world. [2]This is how you can recognize the Spirit of God: Every spirit that acknowledges that Jesus Christ has come in the flesh is from God, [3]but every spirit that does not acknowledge Jesus is not from God. This is the spirit of the antichrist, which you have heard is coming and even now is already in the world.
>
> [4]You, dear children, are from God and have overcome them, because the one who is in you is greater than the one who is in the world. [5]They are from the world and therefore speak from the viewpoint of the world, and the world listens to them. [6]We are from God, and whoever knows God listens to us; but whoever is not from God does not listen to us. This is how we recognize the Spirit of truth and the spirit of falsehood.

[7]Dear friends, let us love one another, for love comes from God. Everyone who loves has been born of God and knows God. [8]Whoever does not love does not know God, because God is love.

We might want to impose a barometer test on the media we allow into our lives; that being, does that message come from God. In so doing, we might restrict the amount of morally damaging content we are faced with day to day.

I would like to repeat one thought from earlier in the book. Please, do not impose conditions on your charity. Charity is your giving love to God. I would not think that you would want God to change in anyway just because you are giving something to Him.

Please read Ephesians 4:1-7

> [1]As a prisoner for the Lord, then, I urge you to live a life worthy of the calling you have received. [2]Be completely humble and gentle; be patient, bearing with one another in love. [3]Make every effort to keep the unity of the Spirit through the bond of peace. [4]There is one body and one Spirit—just as you were called to one hope when you were called— [5]one Lord, one faith, one baptism; [6]one God and Father of all, who is over all and through all and in all.
>
> [7]But to each one of us grace has been given as Christ apportioned it.

The Struggle

Luke 5:1-11

[1]One day as Jesus was standing by the Lake of Gennesaret with the people crowding around him and listening to the word of God, [2]he saw at the water's edge two boats, left there by the fishermen, who were washing their nets. [3]He got into one of the boats, the one belonging to Simon, and asked him to put out a little from shore. Then he sat down and taught the people from the boat.

[4]When he had finished speaking, he said to Simon, "Put out into deep water, and let down the nets for a catch."

[5]Simon answered, "Master, we've worked hard all night and haven't caught anything. But because you say so, I will let down the nets."

[6]When they had done so, they caught such a large number of fish that their nets began to break. [7]So they signaled their partners in the other boat to come and help them, and they came and filled both boats so full that they began to sink.

[8]When Simon Peter saw this, he fell at Jesus' knees and said, "Go away from me, Lord; I am a sinful man!" [9]For he and all his companions were astonished at the catch of fish they had taken, [10]and so were James and John, the sons of Zebedee, Simon's partners.

Then Jesus said to Simon, "Don't be afraid; from now on you will catch men." [11]So they pulled their boats up on shore, left everything and followed him.

I would like to take poetic license and retell this story. There is a gentleman in my Sunday School class, we will call Brian. A few years back he decided to donate some used bikes to a church run center that collects items for needy families, and in this case for Christmas presents. For last Christmas, Brian, and 86 people worked together to bring over 350 bikes to this center.

Brian is a man, just like the rest of us. He goes to work, has a family and attends Sunday School at church. As the word of God is passed on to Brian by our preacher and school teachers, Brian hears a message from Jesus. Jesus presents Brian with an opportunity, a thought to help those families in need to provide for their children at Christmas time.

I am sure that Brian had doubts; "Lord, you are asking me to gather bikes for the needy. This has been tried before and only collected a bike or two. How can this help all of those people in need?"

The Lord told Brian to speak with his friends, put out flyers, gather trucks and drive through various neighborhoods. And, behold, the bikes came to him in great numbers. As the momentum of collections increased, others came to help. For when people see the Lord's will at work, when they see the bounty overflowing, many people want to be bathed in the light of His work.

As the word spread of Brian's accomplishment, many people got involved. The stories of fellowship flowed. The reward for the workers is not the bikes but the warm feelings of God working in their lives.

The Lord and Brian must have had several conversations during this mission. At times, he may have felt unworthy. At times the Lord must have shown His appreciation of Brian's efforts. Their fellowship must be something to see, if it could be shared with us all. But somewhere, I am sure, that God told Brian, "Do not worry about how many bikes and what to do with them for I will provide, understand that now, you too, are a catcher of men."

Brian's mission, more than collecting bikes, more than bringing the light of God to shine on many, but, performing an act so Christ-like, will be spoken about for years to come. What a wonderful legacy to leave for his church, his friends, those that helped out, and, his children.

One way to measure our success at leading a Christ-like life is to visualize what people will say about us once we have passed away, what our legacy will be. I think that you would agree that Brian will continue to leave Christian marks on many people.

Our goal is to behave as much like Christ as we can. It is definitely a struggle. However, it will be how we cope with that struggle, how we deliver on that goal, that we will be remembered by.

How many times have you thought to yourself, or perhaps even heard someone else say something like, "I'm a good person. But, I can't expect to be perfect. I can't make the right choice every time!"

What this tells us is that we do monitor our behavior and our decisions before acting. We do keep our own score card, regardless of how informal that might be. If we can accept that one way in which God speaks to us is through opportunities, and that opportunities are really moment by moment, then we can accept that we are able to decide which path to take and that sometimes, knowingly, we go down the wrong path. Sometimes we choose our will over God's will. I care not to get caught up in percentages of right and wrong decisions. I would prefer us to understand that we have the ability to make the right decisions, and knowledge that if we choose to make the wrong decisions that we have to be responsible for our actions and that path may not prove to be rewarding to us, or for God. But, what I would like us to measure are the times that we are aware of the right decisions to be made and we make them, regardless of what we might consider to be best for us individually at the time.

There Should be No Strangers

If God is love, then there should be no strangers to us in this world. Lofty statement! How do we get to the point of loving every person? Is it possible?

In order to get there, let's see if we can agree on a couple of assumptions; the first assumption being acceptance of the Trinity. Most Christians will agree that there is God, Jesus and the Holy Spirit. Some would disagree that they are all of the same being. Proponents of either side use various sections of the Bible to support their point. Some Biblical quotes supporting the Trinity might include Matthew 28:16-20:

> [16]But the eleven disciples proceeded to Galilee, to the mountain which Jesus had designated. [17]When they saw Him, they worshiped Him; but some were doubtful. [18]And Jesus came up and spoke to them, saying, "All authority has been given to Me in heaven and on earth. [19]Go therefore and make disciples of all the nations, baptizing them in the name of the Father and the Son and the Holy Spirit, [20]teaching them to observe all that I commanded you; and lo, I am with you always, even to the end of the age."

Another might be Matthew 3:16-17:

> [16]After being baptized, Jesus came up immediately from the water; and behold, the heavens were opened, and he saw the Spirit of God descending as a dove and lighting on Him, [17]and behold, a voice out of the heavens said, "This is My beloved Son, in whom I am well-pleased."

The first two quotes above show us that there is God, Jesus and the Holy Spirit. If we look at examples like Genesis 1:26, we see where these three entities are related to each other:

> ^{26}Then God said, "Let Us make man in Our image,
> according to Our likeness; and let them rule over the fish of
> the sea and over the birds of the sky and over the cattle and
> over all the earth, and over every creeping thing that creeps
> on the earth."

A quick note regarding being made in His image: I really don't
think this is meant in the literally sense, as in we look like Him. I
think that it has to do with the image of God as love, as the
acceptor, as grace. Perhaps this might be the Holy Spirit, as in
Him, shared throughout us; a reflection of His Spirit.

It might be easier for us to think of the Trinity as one God in three
people, or entities. At any rate, we will focus on just the Holy
Spirit at the moment. The Holy Spirit is commonly referred to as
that voice we hear inside our heads, perhaps confused with our
conscience. But the Holy Spirit is much more than that. He has
several key initiatives on His agenda. He is here to teach us things
about God and about ourselves in relation to Him. The Holy Spirit
always tells us the truth regardless of whether or not we want to
hear it. He guides us, He convinces us, and if need be, He
commands us. And, as important as all the rest, He prays for us.

It is the mission of the Holy Spirit to reveal Jesus to us. It is the
mission of Jesus to reveal God to us. And, God sent us the Holy
Spirit and Jesus so that we can be brought closer to Him.

The second assumption would be that God is omnipresent. This is
spelled out in Psalm 139, especially verses 7-12:

> ^{7}Where can I go from Your Spirit?
> Or where can I flee from Your presence?
> ^{8}If I ascend to heaven, You are there;
> If I make my bed in Sheol, behold, You are there.
> ^{9}If I take the wings of the dawn,
> If I dwell in the remotest part of the sea,

^{10}Even there Your hand will lead me,
  And Your right hand will lay hold of me.
^{11}If I say, "Surely the darkness will overwhelm me,
  And the light around me will be night,"
^{12}Even the darkness is not dark to You,
  And the night is as bright as the day
  Darkness and light are alike to You.

Now, based on these two assumptions, let's make a leap of faith and look at our Walk in two new ways. The first will deal with communication. The second will deal with a maturation of moving past acting like Jesus and becoming Jesus.

If God is omnipresent, He is everywhere. He sent the Holy Spirit to dwell within us. (1 Corinthians 3:16)

> ^{16}Do you not know that you are a temple of God and that the Spirit of God dwells in you?

And, 1 Corinthians 6:17:

> ^{17}But the one who joins himself to the Lord is one spirit with Him.

And, John 14:16-17:

> ^{16}"I will ask the Father, and He will give you another Helper, that He may be with you forever; ^{17}that is the Spirit of truth, whom the world cannot receive, because it does not see Him or know Him, but you know Him because He abides with you and will be in you."

When you speak with God, how do you carry yourself? Meaning, do you judge Him? Do you belittle Him? Are you sarcastic with Him? Or, do you speak with Him with respect? Even in our worst moments I dare say that most of us speak to Him with respect.

This does not mean we can't be angry or upset or even disappointed. But, bottom line, we are respectful of the Father.

Now, if God is everywhere, if God and the Holy Spirit are one, if the Holy Spirit dwells within each of us, don't we then all have God in us? Our relationship with God requires that we accept God. Depending on our faith, that could be acceptance that God exists, or that God is everywhere, or that God is in us. Then, to the level of our faith and acceptance, how much God do we allow to dwell within us. In some ways this means that we are subjective to Him, in other ways it makes our relationship so much more dynamic. As I first began to think this through, I pictured just a piece of me being God. I would represent that with a closed fist to my chest. Fortunately, a person told me that I could accept more of God; that He could make up all of my spirit. My revelation was that this was exactly what I was trying to reach and I was only putting limitations on myself.

If God makes His presence in all of us, then we should treat everyone else not as a stranger but as God because God, as the Holy Spirit, resides in every person we will speak to. If you have an enemy, if you see a beggar on the street, if you bump into another car in a parking lot, who are all of those other people? They are human vessels that hold the Spirit of God. They are made in His image.

So, now that God is in all of us, how do we communicate with them/Him? What do we say, or more importantly, how do we say what we want to say? How do we listen? What if the other person has yet to accept God, has yet to receive the Holy Spirit in them? Do we treat them differently, even though God is still there inside of them?

We should want to establish a loving, dynamic, respectful, 2-way relationship with God. We should want to be involved in our conversations. We should want to concentrate, to be in the moment, in the present with God. This is how we should be with each other. There really should be no strangers because we should speak to the essence of God in every other person. We need to find the way to see, hear and feel that essence and then communicate to that entity.

Now, for the second, much bigger leap. Let's become Jesus. I am not so arrogant to think that I, or any of us humans, can become Jesus. However, we were made in His image and we have the capability of becoming as loving as Jesus, as nurturing as the Holy Spirit and as accepting as God. What really stops us is our human condition. There is so much to learn while on earth that we can't really become the Jesus that we are capable of. That will come in heaven. But, God has shown us the way.

How did Peter walk on water? Through his faith in Jesus. Jesus told His disciples to go out and heal, to go out and save. How can a mere mortal do those things? Only with the faith that Jesus is in them. Look to John 14:7-14:

> [7]"If you had known Me, you would have known My Father also; from now on you know Him, and have seen Him." [8]Philip said to Him, "Lord, show us the Father, and it is enough for us." [9]Jesus said to him, "Have I been so long with you, and yet you have not come to know Me, Philip? He who has seen Me has seen the Father; how can you say, 'Show us the Father'? [10]Do you not believe that I am in the Father, and the Father is in Me? The words that I say to you I do not speak on My own initiative, but the Father abiding in Me does His works. [11]Believe Me that I am in the Father and the Father is in Me; otherwise believe because of the works themselves. [12]"Truly, truly, I say to you, he who believes in Me, the works that I do, he will do also; and greater works than these he will do; because I go to the Father. [13]Whatever you ask in My name, that will I do, so that the Father may be glorified in the Son. [14]If you ask Me anything in My name, I will do it."

In the passage above, Jesus is telling the disciples that they can perform the same works that He does, that in fact, they can do greater works. There are many stories in the Bible of some of the disciples basically performing miracles after the crucifixion of Jesus. One such story is in Acts 3:1-10:

> [1]Now Peter and John were going up to the temple at the ninth hour, the hour of prayer. [2]And a man who had been lame from his mother's womb was being carried along, whom they used to set down every day at the gate of the temple which is called Beautiful, in order to beg alms of those who were entering the temple. [3]When he saw Peter and John about to go into the temple, he began asking to receive alms. [4]But Peter, along with John, fixed his gaze on him and said, "Look at us!" [5]And he began to give them his attention, expecting to receive something from them. [6]But Peter said, "I do not possess silver and gold, but what I do have I give to you: In the name of Jesus Christ the Nazarene--walk!" [7]And seizing him by the right hand, he raised him up; and immediately his feet and his ankles were strengthened. [8]With a leap he stood upright and began to walk; and he entered the temple with them, walking and leaping and praising God. [9]And all the people saw him walking and praising God; [10]and they were taking note of him as being the one who used to sit at the Beautiful Gate of the temple to beg alms, and they were filled with wonder and amazement at what had happened to him.

How are human beings able to heal a lame man? Yes, Jesus empowered them. But hasn't Jesus empowered all of us. Are we simply falling short in faith and in so doing not having the full impact on others that we could?

Read 1 Corinthians 3:1-3, where Paul says:

> [1]And I, brethren, could not speak to you as to spiritual men, but as to men of flesh, as to infants in Christ. [2]I gave you milk to drink, not solid food; for you were not yet able to receive it. Indeed, even now you are not yet able, [3]for you are still fleshly. For since there is jealousy and strife among you, are you not fleshly, and are you not walking like mere men?

In the last line, Paul is saying that while we toil with our human condition, we can only walk as mere men. Which to me means that if we can tap into God inside of us; if we can learn the lessons Jesus has taught us; if we can submit and allow the Holy Spirit to guide us; then, we can be much more than mere men. Paul has an expectation that the Corinthian people have put limits on their level of Godly love by their immaturity and lack of acceptance of His word.

If we can submit and accept God inside of us, we should be able to see as God sees. We should be able to hear as God hears. We should be able to feel as God feels. How do you walk on water? How do you come to find no strangers? Through faith and through love. Allow God to completely fill the cavity in you that holds your spirit.

Made in the USA
Charleston, SC
09 December 2010